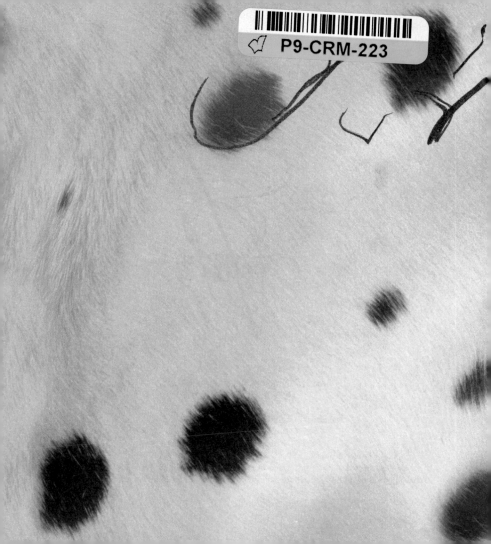

Creative Director: Susie Garland Rice
Design: Colston Rife

Dalmatian Press owns all art and editorial material.
ISBN: 1-57759-269-7
© 1999 Dalmatian Press. All rights reserved.
Printed and bound in the U.S.A. The DALMATIAN PRESS name,
logo and spotted spine are trademarks of Dalmatian Press, Franklin, Tennessee 37067.
Written permission must be secured from the publisher to use or reproduce any part of this book.

10746a/abc's

MY LITTLE BOOK OF
ABC's

Illustrated by Danny Brooks Dalby

Dalmatian Press

Aa

A is for *apple*
so shiny and red.

Bb

B is for *blanket* and also for bed.

Cc

C is for *cat*
who sits all alone.

D is for *dog*
who buried her bone.

Ee E is for *eagle*
who soars through the sky.

F is for *fairy*
who just learned to fly.

Gg

G is for *garden*
that grows
in the
sun.

H is for *hot dog*
to eat on a bun.

I i

I is for *ice cream*
especially strawberry.

J j

J is for *jack-o'-lantern* who looks pretty scary.

K k

K is for *kitten*
who's ready to eat.

Ll L is for *lollipop*
that tastes so sweet.

Mm

M is for *mouse*
in a red jumpsuit.

N is for *nose*
that looks quite cute.

Nn

O is for *owl*
a fellow who's wise.

P is for *pudding*
and also peach pies.

Qq

Q is for *quail*
who loves to sing.

R is for *rabbit*
who wears a ring.

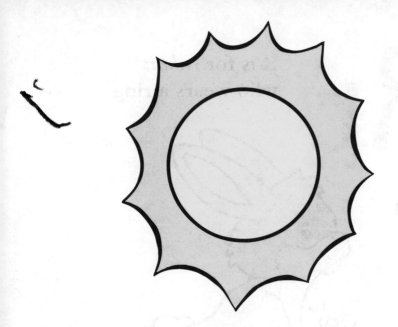

Ss

S is for *sun*
it has a warm glow.

Tt

T is for *turtle*
who's really quite slow.

Uu

U is for *umbrella*
it keeps off the rain.

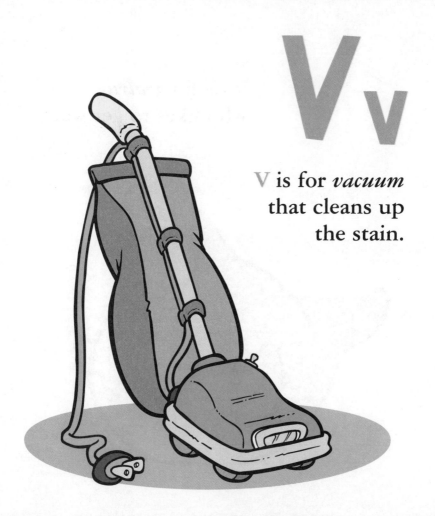

V is for *vacuum*
that cleans up
the stain.

Ww

W is for *walrus*
who likes to get wet.

Then comes X, Y, and Z
and that's the alphabet.

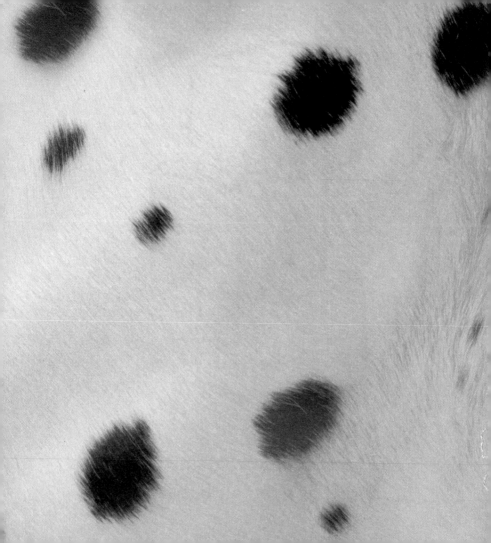